Thoughts of You, My Friend

A collection of poems on friendship
Edited by Susan Polis Schutz

D0962774

Blue Mountain Press ™

Boulder, Colorado

Library of Congress Number: 82-72631
ISBN: 0-88396-180-6

Manufactured in the United States of America.
First Printing: September, 1982.
Second Printing: August, 1983.

The following works have appeared previously
in Blue Mountain Arts publications:

"Since I've known you," and "It's partly because of you," by
Andrew Tawney. Copyright © Blue Mountain Arts, Inc., 1982.
"A friendship as cherished as ours," by Andrew Tawney;
and "Being friends comes so naturally to us," by Jamie
Delere. Copyright © Blue Mountain Arts, Inc., 1981. "It takes
more than words," by Susan Polis Schutz. Copyright ©
Stephen Schutz and Susan Polis Schutz, 1981. All rights reserved.

Thanks to the Blue Mountain Arts creative staff.

ACKNOWLEDGMENTS appear on page 62.

Blue Mountain Press INC.

P.O. Box 4549, Boulder, Colorado 80306

CONTENTS

Everyone needs at least one good,
    close friend;
one who means a lot,
and who can share secrets and feelings
that might otherwise be
locked up and afraid to come out.
Everyone needs someone
who cares — and doesn't hide it;
someone to ease the down moods.
Thank you . . . for being the one for me.
I hope my friendship has been
at least half as good for you,
because friends as special as you
are hard to find.

— Barbara Gladys

You are always
     my friend
when I am happy
or when I am sad
when I am all alone
or when I am with people
You are always my friend
if I see you today
or if I see you
     a year from now
if I talk to you today
or if I talk to you
     a year from now
You are always my friend
and though through the years
we will change
it doesn't matter what I do
or it doesn't matter what you do
Throughout our lifetime
you are always my friend

— Susan Polis Schutz

Since I've known you
I've become aware
of a change in myself . . .
I think I've become
a little more open
and more confident,
more caring and more aware
of the world around me.
Maybe it's because
I've admired those traits in you,
and because you've made me feel
that I deserve
more smiles than frowns,
more sunlight than shade . . .

You deserve
so much more than I can give you,
but for now
I'll just say thanks
for being
such a wonderful friend.

— Andrew Tawney

I'd like to capture a rainbow
and stick it in a big box
so that,
anytime you wanted to,
you could reach in and pull out
a piece of sunshine.

I'd like to build you a mountain
that you could call your very own —
a place to find serenity
in those times when you
feel the need to be
closer to yourself.

I'd like to be the one
who's there with you when you're
lonely or troubled
or you just need
someone
to hold on to.

I'd like to do all this and more
to make your life happy.

But sometimes
it isn't easy to do
the things I would like to do
or give the things I would
like to give.

So . . . until I learn how to
catch rainbows and build mountains,
let me do for you
    that which I know best . . .

        . . . Let me simply
        be your friend.

— Jacqueline J. Hancock

It's not often
that we get the chance
to tell our friends
        how much we care,
    and how much they mean to us.
But what better time
than today . . .
to tell a friend like you.

I can only hope
that you will somehow know
that these words
really do come
from the bottom of my heart.

                    — Karen Meditz

I have been blessed to have a friendship
        like ours.
You have seen me at my worst
        and best,
you've held me when I was in despair
and laughed with me when I was happy.
Our friendship has truly been blessed
        by God
because it is unconditional.
I love you, and will always treasure
the word friend —
        because of you.

— Jan Kirkley Boyd

You are my best friend
because you feel so much
        like home to me . . .
that feeling that someone cares;
that feeling of welcome
that the sight of home
        always brings.

With you as my friend,
I can always know sunshine
        more than my troubles.
You turn any sadness
into a simple understanding
        that I can accept.
And when I'm feeling happy . . .
and wanting to share everything
that is wonderful to me,
you are there . . . ready to listen.

You add so much
to each day . . .
and I wanted to say "thanks"
for being my best friend.

— Yvonne

17

I think of you
as a very special, dear friend . . .
in a place I hold in my heart
        for just a very few.
You came into my life
    offering happiness
    with caring underneath,
and I find myself responding
    in the same manner.
It is so easy to talk with you
    about things that sometimes are hard,
    and about things that sometimes I
    have kept well hidden . . .
            even from myself . . .

You seem to be able to draw that out of me,
    and I think that maybe
        I am able to do that for you.
What a beautiful way
    to have
        and build
            a friendship.

— Sue Mitchell

Friend . . .
Who you are and what you
                    mean to me
are expressions of what
                    life means to me.
I am thankful that in this time
                    our paths merge.
Only the future knows
how long we will travel the same ways,
certain only that our lives will be changed
because of our common experiences.
Let's enjoy the walk together
                    and celebrate
the person each of us brings to the journey
and the friends we are becoming
along the way.

— Nancy Ferrell

It takes more than words
to let you know
how much it means to me
to have you as a friend
I can depend on you for understanding
when I am confused
I can depend on you for comfort
when I am sad
I can depend on you for laughter
when I am happy
I am so thankful to know that you are
always my friend

— Susan Polis Schutz

Whenever I am in need
of a kind word, a gentle touch
    or a reassuring look,
you are always
    there for me.
And it all comes so
very naturally for you . . .
your caring ways and
your way of saying
    "You matter to me."
I often think how lucky I am
to have a friend as wonderful as you.

— Karen S. Clark

Today
I thought about you
and about what our friendship
means to me.
About how we give
    each other encouragement.
We can sense a longing.
We listen
to each other's inner thoughts
    with love and concern,
and without giving
            any judgment.
We try to comfort
each other's hurts.
But best of all,
we can find companionship,
even in silence.

Our friendship
        means a lot to me.

— Doris Amundson Arnold

Regardless of
whom I meet
or what I do
or what I have become
it is the friends
I grew up with
that I feel
closest to
and that I have
the most in common with
Though we don't see
each other often
when we do
it is as though
we were always together —
so comfortable
so natural
so honest
I guess old friends
who know where we come from
who know our backgrounds
who know our families
have an understanding
of us
that no new friend
can ever have

— Susan Polis Schutz

Each of us yearns for a heart
   that beats in unison with our own;
for an ear to which we can
pour out our confidences and troubles,
for a hand we can safely grasp,
for an arm we can always lean on.

But it is not only when difficulties arise
that we know the value of a trusted friend;
but even in our most bright and happy hours,
we feel that joys
   have not half their sweetness
unless we have a companion
   to share them with us.
Whether our dwelling be a
   castle or a cabin,
our trials will be lighter
and our comforts will be richer
if we have a true friend.

— Thain Davidson

There is truth
and simplicity
in genuine friendship.

— Cicero

I cherish my friends,
for I know that
of all things
granted us . . .
none is greater
  or better
    than friendship.

— Pietro Aretino
1537 A.D.

My love and friendship for you
have become so dear to me . . .
I want to hold a place in your heart
as you hold one in mine,
whether we are on separate ends
    of God's earth
    or close together;
let us not grow apart
or let any separation
too large to bridge
    ever come between us;
time passes too quickly
    to spend it on anything
    but well-being . . .

Dearest of friends,
I hope that you will be
happy with every moment of life,
    every breath,
    every touch,
    every sight, smell and sound.
This is my wish of happiness for you,
and my way of saying
"I love you."
May your dreams
    never disappear with age,
but may they continue
as alive and as beautiful as you
with the knowledge that they
will someday come true.

— Joanne Domenech

Friendship is giving
a helping hand
during a moment of need.
It is the sharing of
memories after years
of fun and adventure together.
Friendship speaks honestly
when called upon
and kindly without asking.
It is the greatest of life's
many pleasures
and can only be appreciated
with another.
I am grateful to you for
teaching me the many
joys that are part of
our friendship.

— E. Lori Milton

If you need a friend
to talk with,
come to me.
I will listen to you speak.

If you need a friend
to walk with,
come to me.

If you need a friend
to laugh with,
come to me.
I will share
        in your happiness.

If you need a friend
to cry with,
come to me.
I will try
     to cure your sadness.

I am here if you need me.
I am your friend.

— Jillien Cruse

I am always so glad
when you tell me
what fills your world
and of the courses your dreams
   are taking you . . .
You must understand
that it is only natural for me
to have an interest
            in what you do,
for wherever you go —
my heart
         goes with you.

— Kele Daniels

A friendship as cherished as ours
is more than just a closeness of two people . . .
it's an endearing bond felt and given,
and one of the most
important aspects of our lives.

A friendship
as secure as ours
is more than just a feeling . . .
it's a knowing and a being,
a knowledge that each will
always be there for the other
for as long as time will allow
and as strong as our hearts will permit . . .

A friendship
as rewarding as ours
is more than just an experience . . .
it's an event that is shared
by two fortunate people,
given the opportunity to
travel together through this
journey of life.

A friendship
as abundant as ours
is the most beautiful present
you could offer me
and the greatest gift
I could ever receive.

— Andrew Tawney

Sometimes when I am
  really down, and nobody
seems to be my friend,
I think of you
  and the gentlest eyes
    I've ever seen,
  the warmest smile,
  the most accepting heart.
I think of what you mean to me
and before long . . .
the skies of living
are clear again
and the sun of hope
is warm.

— Mary Shader

So often I sit and think
about the way things were
The fun and friends,
the joy we all had
  and the times of just being together . . .
Of course there were some days,
times we wondered how we made it.
But our friendship helped us through.

Now we may be separated,
but the bond is still there.
Friendship holds us
            together.

— Joyce Brink

Being friends
comes so naturally to us —
We're always there for each other,
and it's never a chore, it's done
                    from desire;
never an effort, but always a pleasure.
We've been friends
for quite awhile now,
and I'm sure that you know what I mean
when I say that
    the memories that we've got
are some of the finest I ever
                    hope to have . . .

It makes me glad to think
that you'll be with me
   and I'll be with you
      as friends . . .
to face the new times ahead,
to share the wonders they will bring,
to confront whatever trials
               they may hold.
It's nice to know
you'll always have me
caring for you,
and I'll always have you
      just a thought away.

— Jamie Delere

I simply want you
to know how nice
things have been
since I met you,
how very special it is
to spend time with you,
and how much better
    life seems
with you in my world.

— Rowland R. Hoskins, Jr.

You've been more to me than a friend . . .
We've shared more than most people do —
    feelings that time won't erase
No words can ever let you know
    the peace I feel when you are near
In times of trouble, your eyes express
    exactly what I need to hear
In times of joy, your smile says
    you're sharing what I feel
In times of doubt, I always knew
    I could trust in your loyalty
We've stood the test across the miles
    and watched our friendship grow
I've come to learn, when it comes to friends,
    there's no one quite like you.

— Marie Grady Palcic

You're that special kind of friend
that everyone wishes they could have.
I always know when we're apart
        that we're still so close,
and when we're together
our time will be spent
            enjoying it to the fullest.

It's not everyone that can
        have a special friend
            like you.
I'm proud to say
            that I do.

— Teresa M. Fox

Good friends are rare.
I am happy to say that
you are a "friend" to me,
for it is a word
to which I attach
a great deal
of importance.

— Paul Gauguin

Sometimes I wish
you would tell me
what you're thinking
    no matter
how sad or angry . . .
for even though
I like to laugh with you,
we shouldn't hide behind
a smile when things are wrong . . .
I care for you
whether you're happy or sad . . .
I'm your friend.

— Laura West

Just knowing that your thoughts
   are with me
Warms me when I'm cold . . .
Remembering your gentle touch
Soothes away my tears.

The miles between us
   keep us strong . . .
A strength that brings visions
   of times yet to be shared
By special friends
like
   us.

— Joseph R. Shaver

You have touched somewhere inside me,
    and helped me believe in my dreams.
You draw them out of their hiding places,
    and give me the courage
    to think that just maybe
        they're really possible.
What more can anyone do for another,
        than to help him learn
        to believe in himself?
You must know . . .
        that I owe you so much . . .

— Sue Mitchell

Friendship defies age
and ignores distance.
It weathers the hard times
and shares the good.
Together we have found this.
Our friendship has provided
   acceptance
and understanding in a world
that pushes people apart.
But I will always remain
with the memories
of the times we have shared
knowing how fortunate I am
to be able to call you my friend.

— Cindy Yrun

To have a friend is to have one of
the sweetest gifts; to be a friend is
to experience a solemn and tender
education of soul from day to day.
A friend remembers us when we have
forgotten ourselves. A friend may
praise us and we are not embarrassed.
He takes loving heed of our work,
our health, our aims, our plans.
He may rebuke us and we are not
angry. If he is silent, we understand.
It takes a great soul to be a friend . . .
One must forgive much, forget
much, forbear much. It costs time,
affection, strength, patience, love.
Sometimes a man must lay down
his life for his friends. There is no true
friendship without self-sacrifice.
We will be slow to make friends, but
having once made them, neither life
nor death, misunderstanding, distance
nor doubt must ever come between.

— Anonymous

You are a very
giving person.

For that reason
it is so easy
to want to give to you
in return.

— jonivan

You're not afraid to look at me
and say the truth
that I don't want to hear . . .
and I don't argue
or turn away
because I know you are right . . .
and I'm relieved at your honesty . . .
and I'm glad that you're my friend.

— bonnie lee harris

Security in friendship
sustains my life.
To reach out, sensing your presence
        is indeed a precious gift.
Never alone, my strength endures.
In quiet times, I hear your heart and soul.
We have passed all the tests
                of distance and time.
Thank you, my friend . . .
for being my friend.

— Sabrina Renee Fair

Having a friend
like you . . . who is
so much like me,
makes me think that no
two people could be
as close in spirit
as we are.
You make me appreciate
     who I am,
more than ever before.
You showed me,
just by being you,
how essential it is
to like one's self.

— Janice Lamb

Being a friend
comes naturally.
It is taking a moment
     out of your life
to give of yourself
by bringing comfort,
     encouragement and peace.

     You do it graciously . . .
          and I thank you.

— Linda DuPuy Moore

It's partly because of you
and the special qualities you've got
that I've tried to be
    a better person myself.
Your sincerity,
your good natured attitude,
your optimism and your strengths . . .
all those things that have
given me a certain outlook
and a special way
of approaching life.
Having you in my days . . .
    knowing you as I do,
has helped me over the rough spots
    and through the difficult times.
I feel like I owe you a lot . . .
but can repay you
    with so little.
But as little as I have to give,
it would mean so much to me
    just for you to know
that you've added to my days
and given life
    a special glow.

                        — Andrew Tawney

57

Happiness . . .
is time spent with a friend
and looking forward
to sharing time with them
again.

— Lee Wilkinson

A Lifetime Friendship

Though we don't see each other very much
nor do we write to each other very much
nor do we phone each other very much
I always know that, at any time,
I could call, write or see you
and everything would be exactly the same
You would understand everything I am saying
and everything that I am thinking

Our friendship does not depend
on being together
It is deeper than that
Our closeness is something inside of us
that is always there
ready to be shared with each other
whenever the need arises

It is such a comfortable
    and warm feeling
to know that we have such
    a lifetime
        friendship

— Susan Polis Schutz

ACKNOWLEDGMENTS

We gratefully acknowledge the permission granted by the following authors, publishers and authors' representatives to reprint poems and excerpts from their publications.

Barbara Gladys for "Everyone needs at least," by Barbara Gladys. Copyright © Barbara Gladys, 1981. All rights reserved. Reprinted by permission.

Jacqueline J. Hancock for "I'd like to capture a rainbow," by Jacqueline J. Hancock. Copyright © Jacqueline J. Hancock, 1982. All rights reserved. Reprinted by permission.

Karen Meditz for "It's not often," by Karen Meditz. Copyright © Karen Meditz, 1982. All rights reserved. Reprinted by permission.

Jan Kirkley Boyd for "I have been blessed," by Jan Kirkley Boyd. Copyright © Jan Kirkley Boyd, 1982. All rights reserved. Reprinted by permission.

Yvonne for "You are my best friend," by Yvonne. Copyright © Yvonne, 1982. All rights reserved. Reprinted by permission.

Sue Mitchell for "I think of you," by Sue Mitchell. Copyright © Sue Mitchell, 1981. And for "You have touched somewhere inside me," by Sue Mitchell. Copyright © Sue Mitchell, 1982. All rights reserved. Reprinted by permission.

Nancy Ferrell for "Friend . . .," by Nancy Ferrell. Copyright © Nancy Ferrell, 1981. All rights reserved. Reprinted by permission.

Karen S. Clark for "Whenever I am in need," by Karen S. Clark. Copyright © Karen S. Clark, 1982. All rights reserved. Reprinted by permission.

Doris Amundson Arnold for "Today I thought about you," by Doris Amundson Arnold. Copyright © Doris Amundson Arnold, 1981. All rights reserved. Reprinted by permission.

Joanne Domenech for "My love and friendship for you," by Joanne Domenech. Copyright © Joanne Domenech, 1982. All rights reserved. Reprinted by permission.

E. Lori Milton for "Friendship is giving," by E. Lori Milton. Copyright © E. Lori Milton, 1982. All rights reserved. Reprinted by permission.

Jillien Cruse for "If you need a friend," by Jillien Cruse. Copyright © Jillien Cruse, 1982. All rights reserved. Reprinted by permission.

Kele Daniels for "I am always so glad,' by Kele Daniels. Copyright © Kele Daniels, 1982. All rights reserved. Reprinted by permission.

Mary Shader for "Sometimes when I am really down," by Mary Shader. Copyright © Mary Shader, 1981. All rights reserved. Reprinted by permission.

Joyce Brink for "So often I sit and think," by Joyce Brink. Copyright © Joyce Brink, 1981. All rights reserved. Reprinted by permission.

Rowland R. Hoskins, Jr., for "I simply want you," by Rowland R. Hoskins, Jr. Copyright © Rowland R. Hoskins, Jr., 1981. All rights reserved. Reprinted by permission.

Marie Grady Palcic for "You've been more to me than a friend," by Marie Grady Palcic. Copyright © Marie Grady Palcic, 1982. All rights reserved. Reprinted by permission.

Teresa M. Fox for "You're that special kind of friend," by Teresa M. Fox. Copyright © Teresa M. Fox, 1981. All rights reserved. Reprinted by permission.

Laura West for "Sometimes I wish," by Laura West. Copyright © Laura West, 1981. All rights reserved. Reprinted by permission.

Joseph R. Shaver for "Just knowing that your thoughts," by Joseph R. Shaver. Copyright © Joseph R. Shaver, 1982. All rights reserved. Reprinted by permission.